piano • vocal • guitar

# DIANE BIRCH
## bible belt

D0504044

ISBN 978-1-4234-9186-6

## HAL•LEONARD®
## CORPORATION
7777 W. BLUEMOUND RD. P.O. BOX 13819 MILWAUKEE, WI 53213

In Australia Contact:
**Hal Leonard Australia Pty. Ltd.**
4 Lentara Court
Cheltenham, Victoria, 3192 Australia
Email: ausadmin@halleonard.com.au

Visit Hal Leonard Online at
**www.halleonard.com**

# contents

# FIRE ESCAPE

Words and Music by
DIANE BIRCH

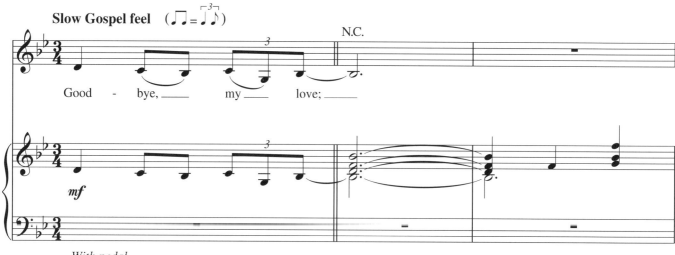

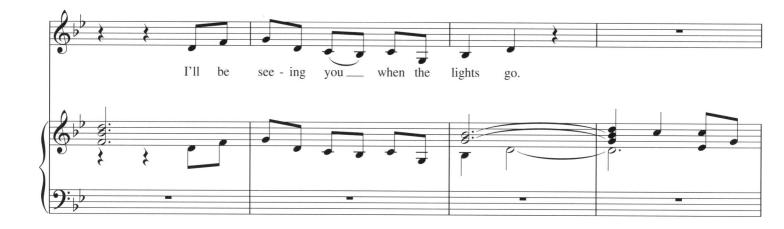

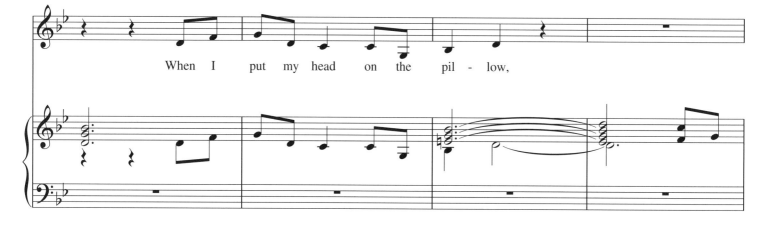

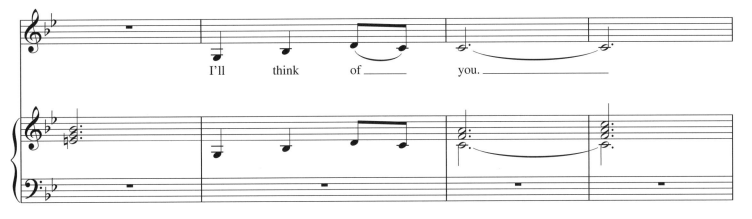

I'll think of ____ you. _____

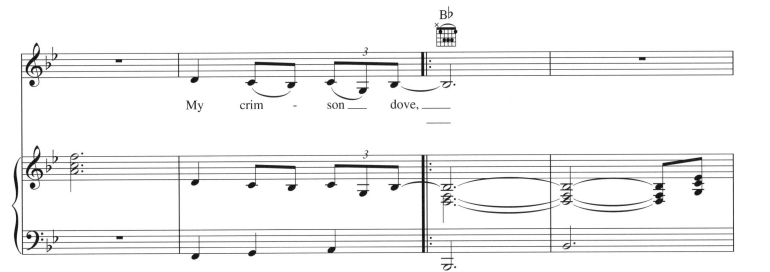

My crim - son ____ dove, ____

Bb

I wish that I could save you from the sad - ness.
it ain't gon - na be the same with - out you.

Gm

Hon - ey, all a - round me lies the
Aw, ____ think of all the shit we've

**C7**

mad - ness,
been through.

ooh, _____ of _____
Ooh, _____ I know, _____

**F7**

___ your ___ love. _____
___ I ___ know. _____

**Dm7**          **Gm7**

What makes the price       good e - nough to wan - na
Love makes the price       good e - nough to wan - na

*3. Instrumental solo*          *Both times:* (Oooh, ___ oooh, ___ oooh, ___

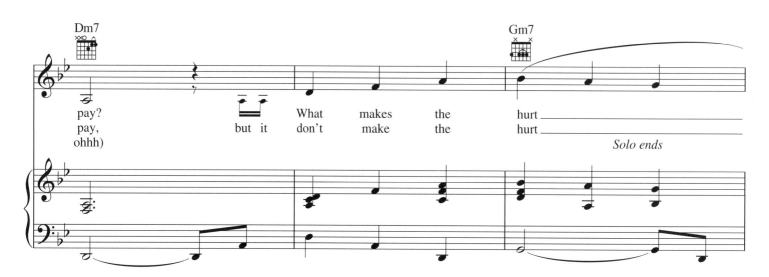

**Dm7**          **Gm7**

pay?       What makes the       hurt _____
pay,   but it don't makes the   hurt _____
ohhh)                    *Solo ends*

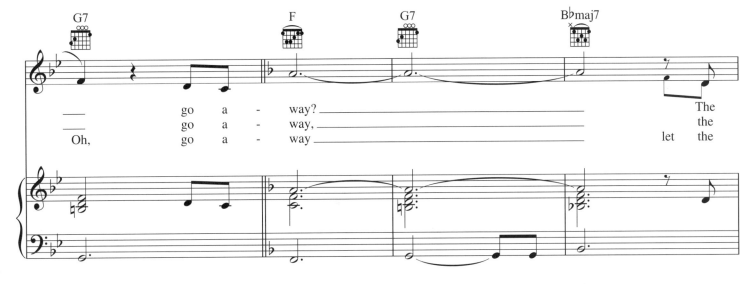

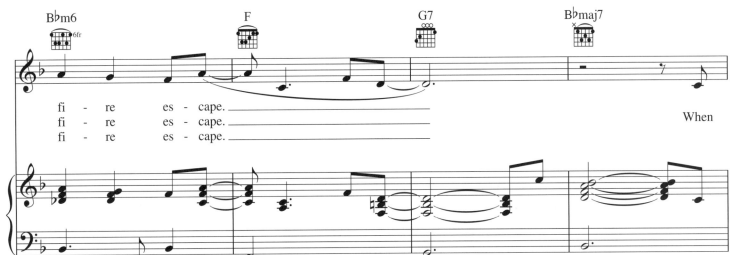

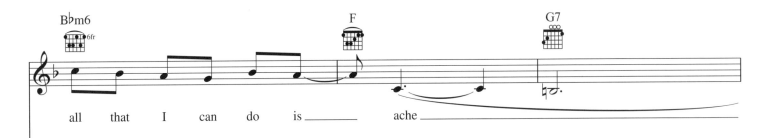

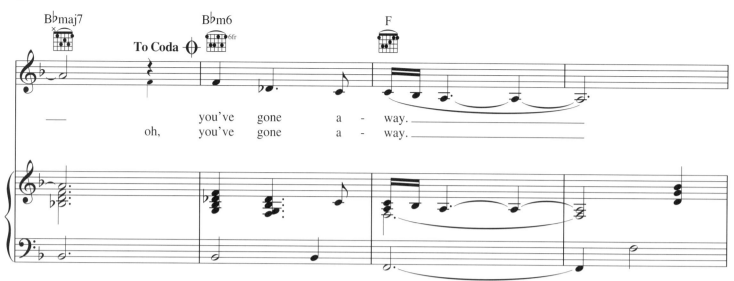

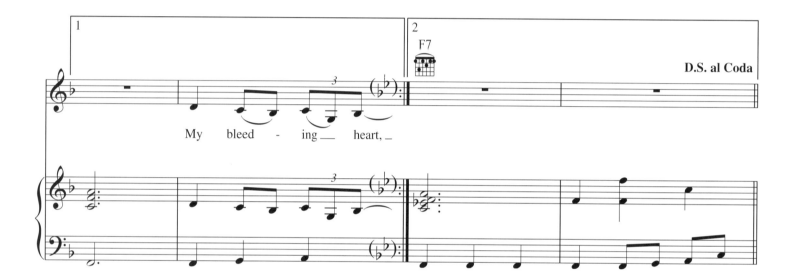

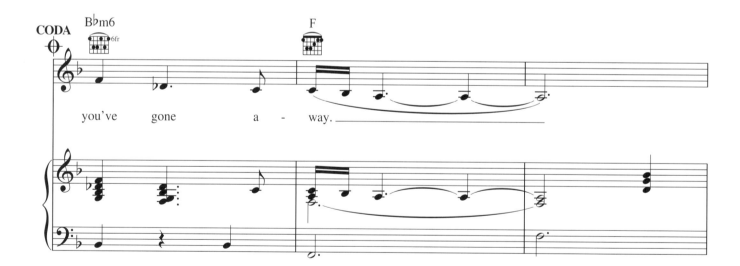

# VALENTINO

Words and Music by
DIANE BIRCH

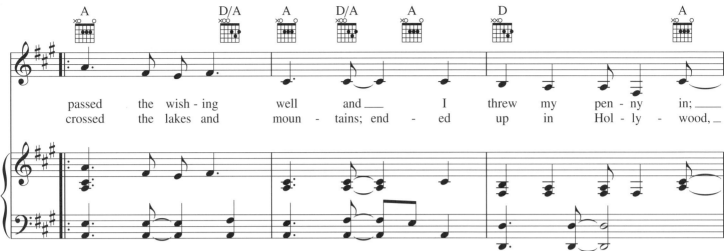

passed the wish - ing well and \_\_ I threw my pen - ny in; \_\_
crossed the lakes and moun - tains; end - ed up in Hol - ly - wood, \_\_

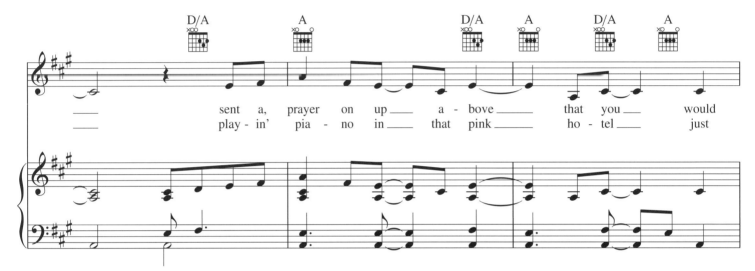

\_\_ sent a, prayer on up \_\_ a - bove \_\_ that you \_\_ would
\_\_ play - in' pia - no in \_\_ that pink \_\_ ho - tel \_\_ just

come my way \_\_ a - gain. \_\_ Yeah, I've
like you said I \_\_ would. \_\_ I kept

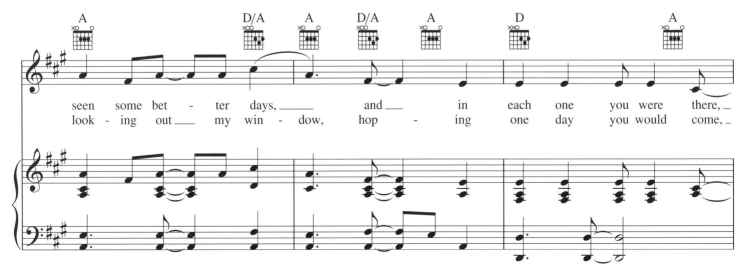

seen some bet - ter days, \_\_ and \_\_ in each one you were there, \_\_
look - ing out \_\_ my win - dow, hop - ing one day you would come, \_\_

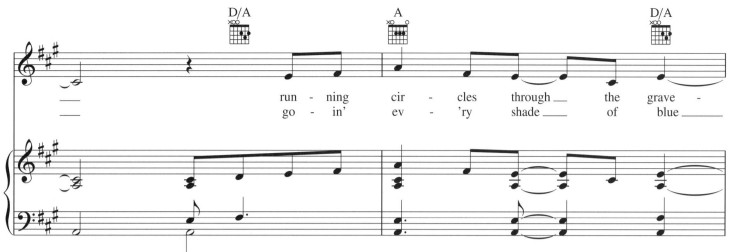

run - ning    cir - cles    through ___ the    grave -
go - in'    ev - 'ry    shade ___ of    blue ___

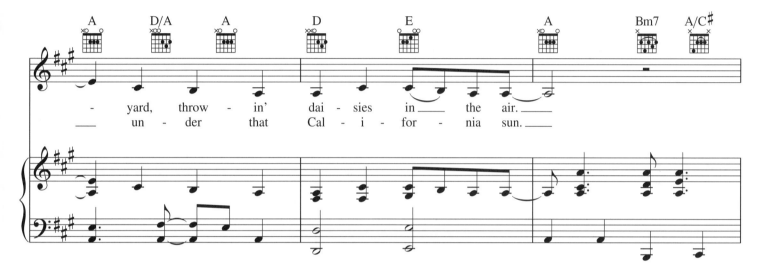

- yard,    throw - in'    dai - sies    in ___ the    air. ___
___ un - der    that    Cal - i - for - nia    sun. ___

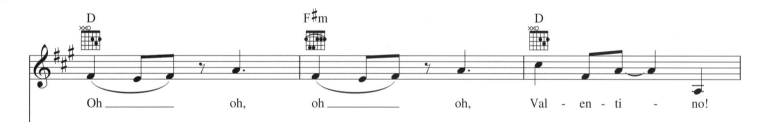

Oh _____ oh,    oh _____ oh,    Val - en - ti - no!

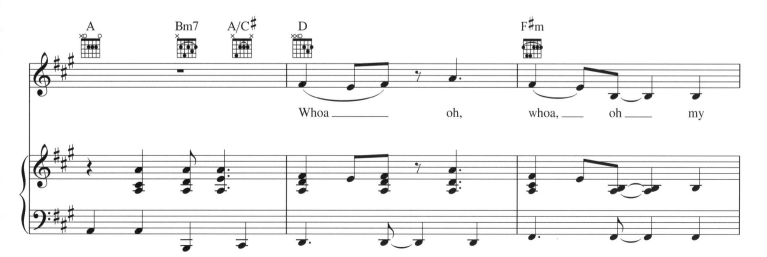

Whoa _____ oh,    whoa, ___ oh ___ my

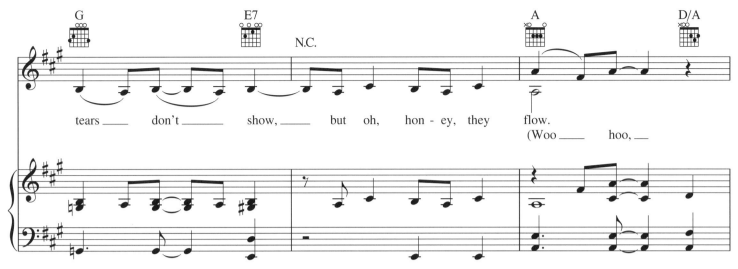

tears _____ don't _____ show, _____ but oh, hon - ey, they flow.
(Woo _____ hoo, _____

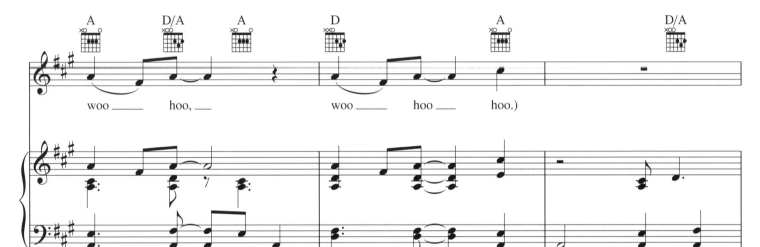

woo _____ hoo, _____ woo _____ hoo _____ hoo.)

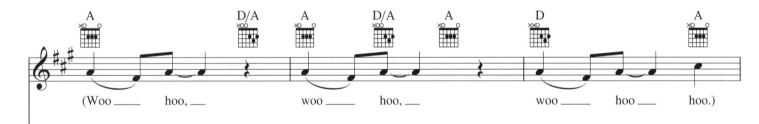

(Woo _____ hoo, _____ woo _____ hoo, _____ woo _____ hoo _____ hoo.)

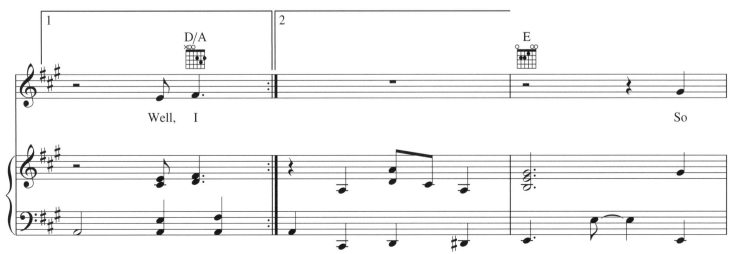

Well, I                                                                                    So

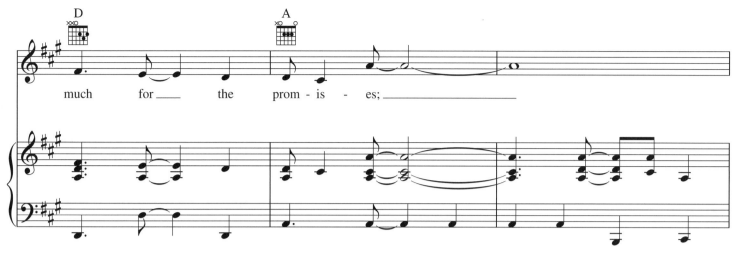

much for \_\_\_\_ the prom - is - es; _____

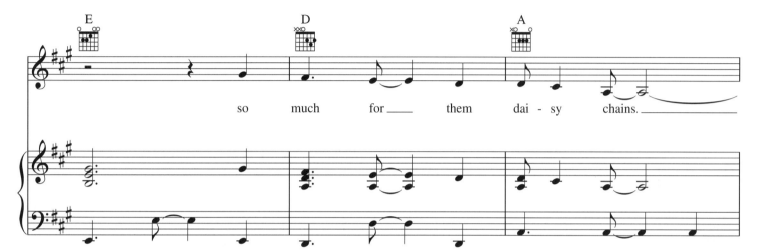

so much for \_\_\_\_ them dai - sy chains. _____

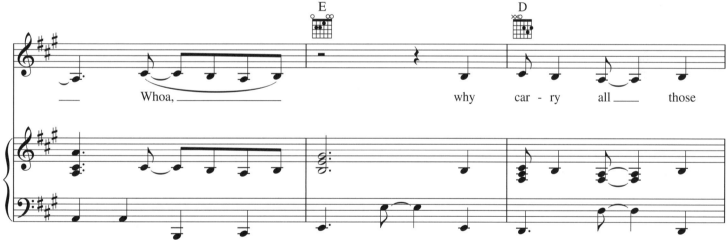

\_\_\_ Whoa, _____ why car - ry all \_\_\_ those

heav - y dreams \_\_\_\_\_ when the on - ly one \_\_\_ I

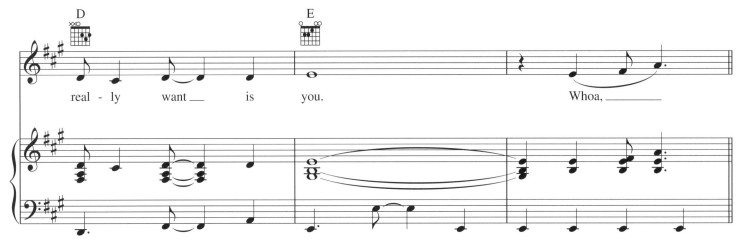

real - ly want ___ is you. Whoa, _____

oh, _____ Val - en - ti - no!
flow. _____

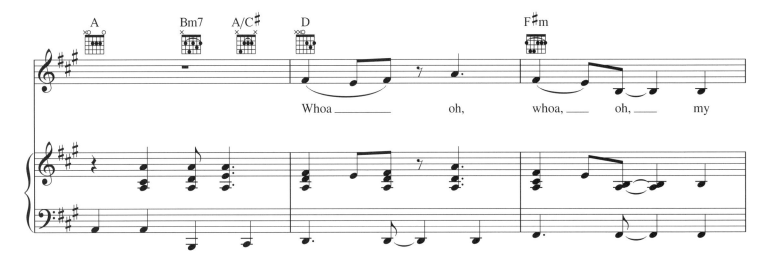

Whoa _____ oh, whoa, ___ oh, ___ my

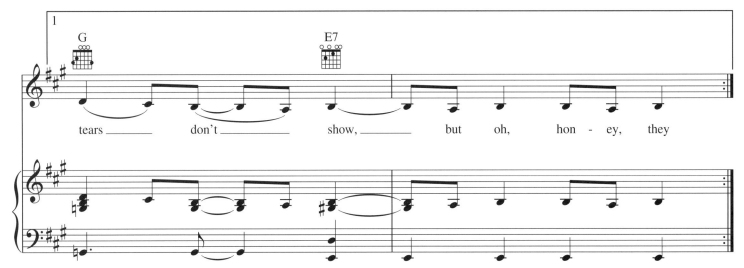

tears _____ don't _____ show, _____ but oh, hon - ey, they

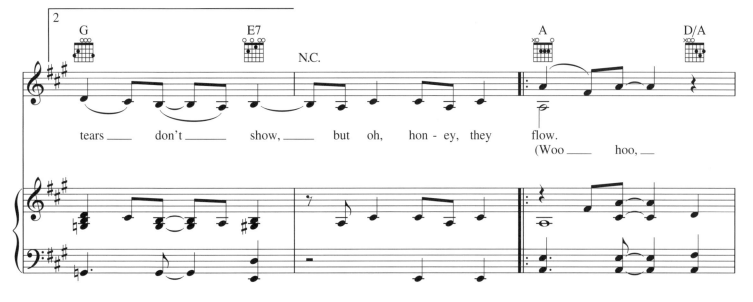

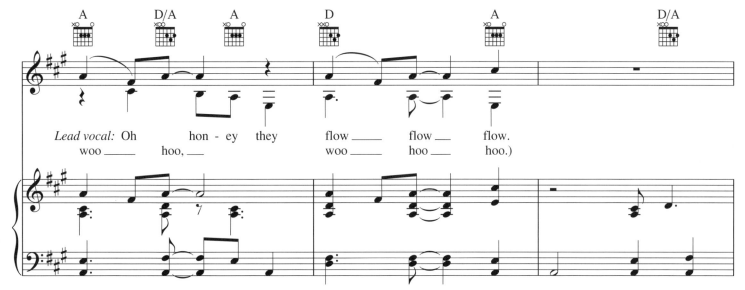

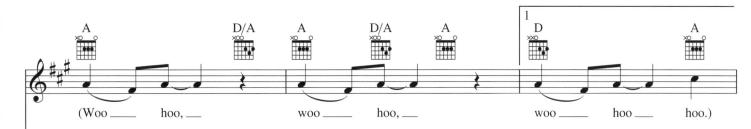

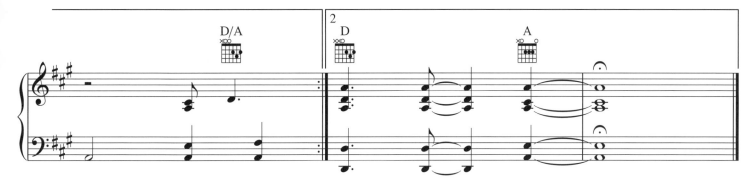

# FOOLS

Words and Music by
DIANE BIRCH

* Recorded a half step lower.

tell - in' me to change ___ my ___ ways. ___ Well, I know
tell - in' me my dream's ___ gone ___ cold. ___ Well, I know

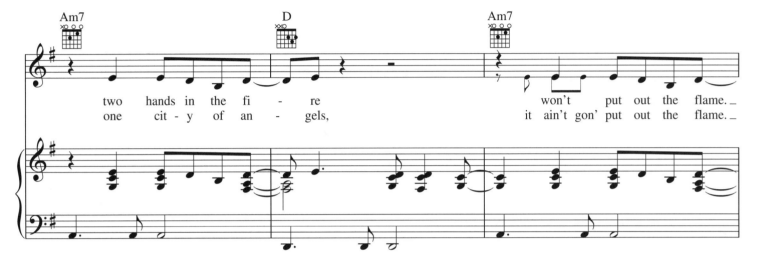

two hands in the fi - re won't put out the flame. ___
one cit - y of an - gels, it ain't gon' put out the flame. ___

Yeah, I got your num -
Ooh, my love is a fi -

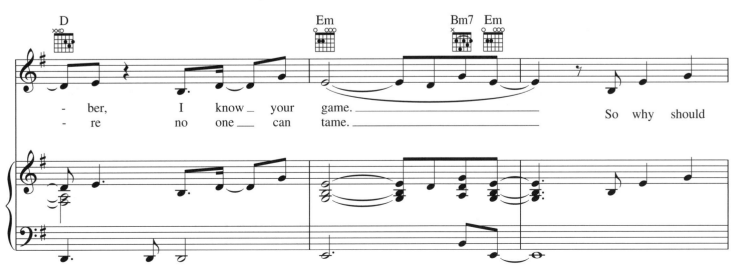

- ber, I know ___ your game. ___ So why should
- re no one ___ can tame. ___

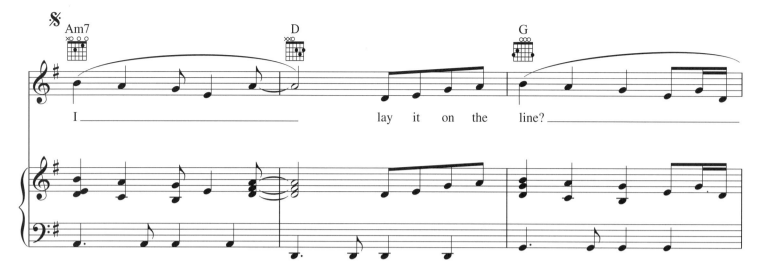

I _____ lay it on the line? _____

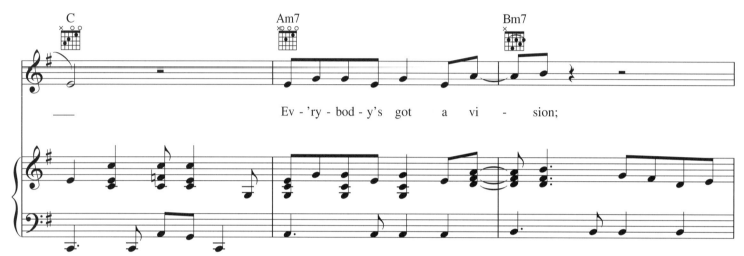

___ Ev - 'ry - bod - y's got a vi - sion;

ev - 'ry - bod - y's got a plan. ___ You tell me lies; _____

___ you look me in the eyes. _____ Well,

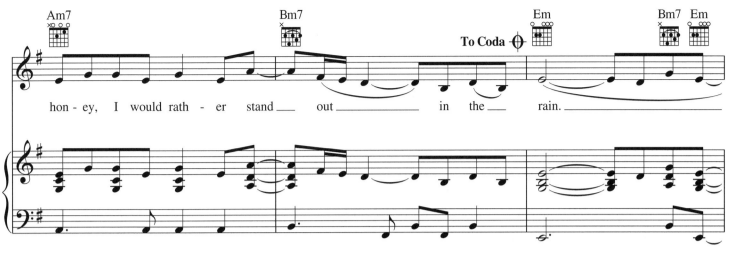

hon - ey, I would rath - er stand ___ out ___ in the ___ rain. ___

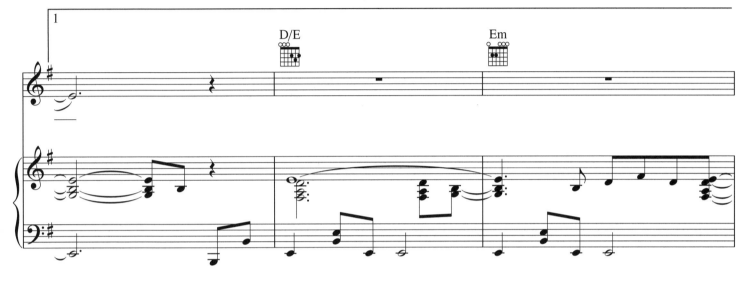

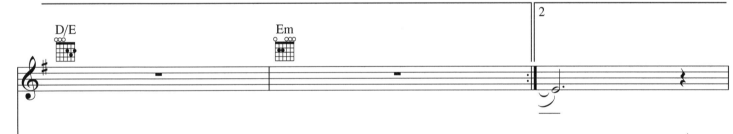

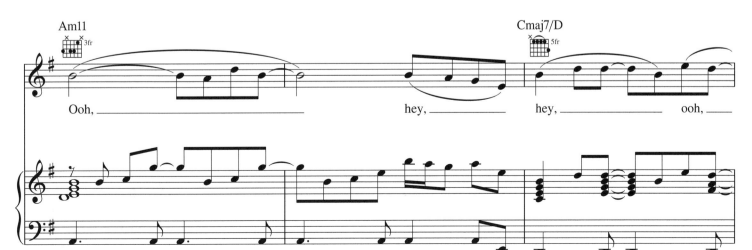

Ooh, ___ hey, ___ hey, ___ ooh, ___

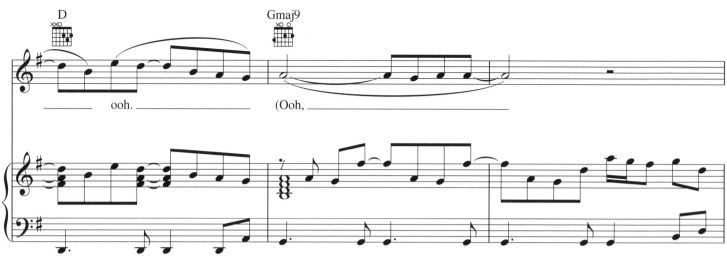

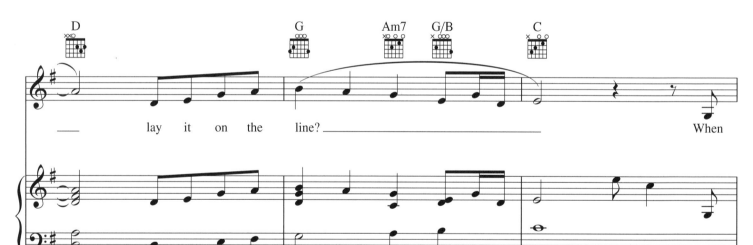

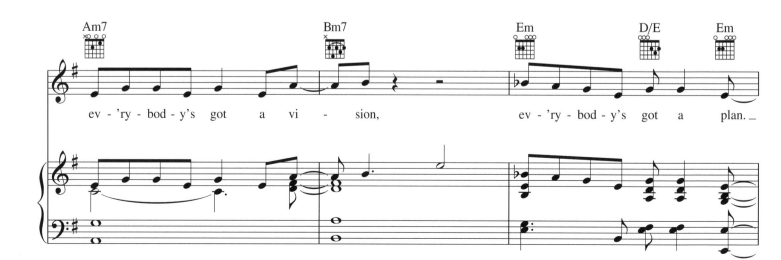

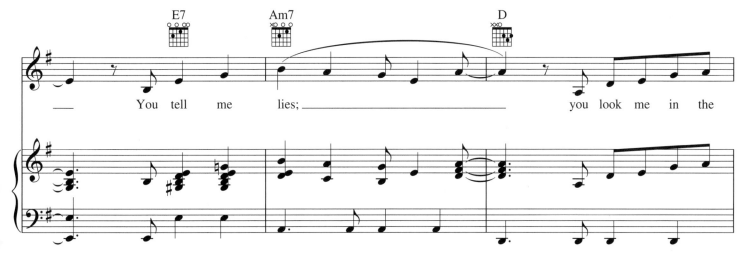

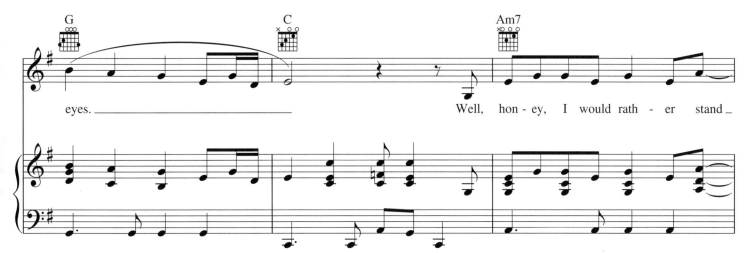

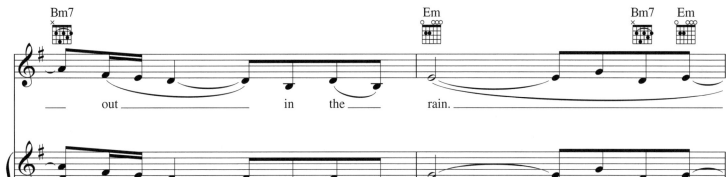

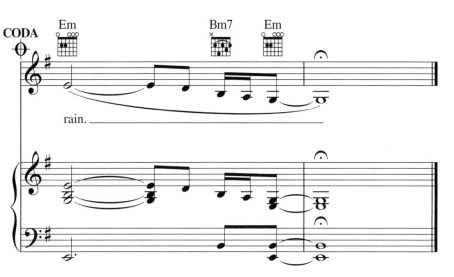

# NOTHING BUT A MIRACLE

Words and Music by
DIANE BIRCH

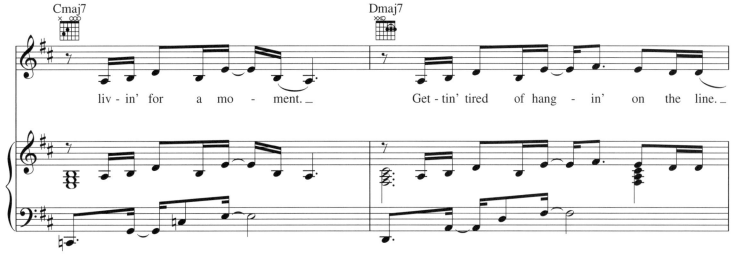

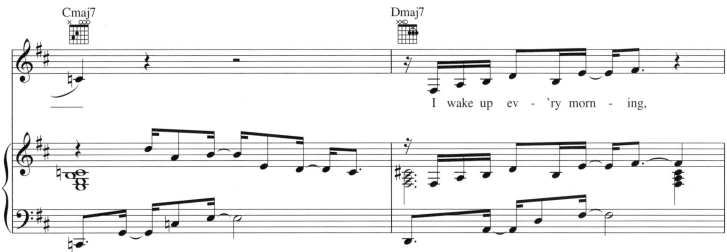

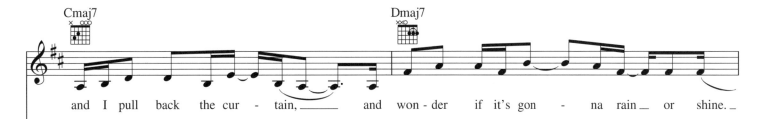

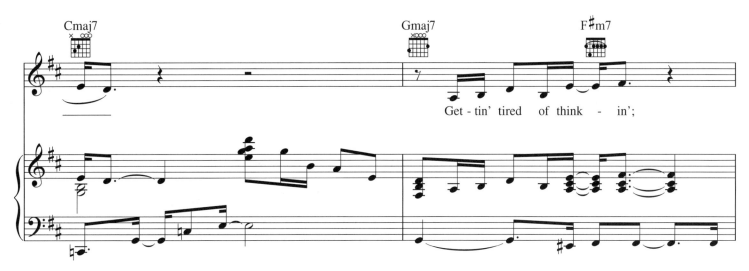

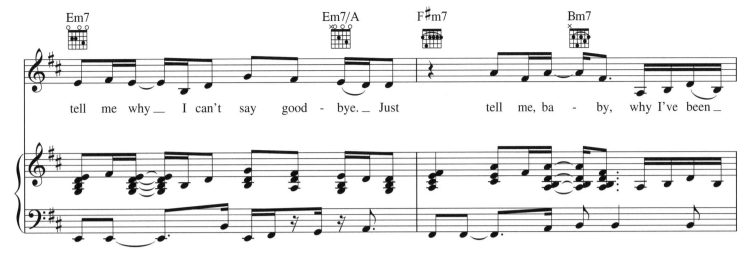

tell me why __ I can't say good - bye. __ Just tell me, ba - by, why I've been __

hold - ing on __ for so long; __ and noth - in' but a mir - a - cle is gon - na

bring ya back, __ bring ya back __ to me now. _____ Whoa, __ whoa,

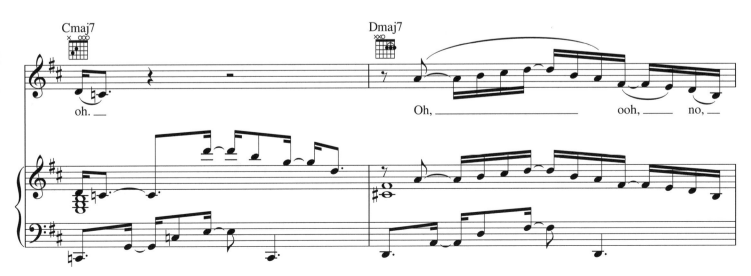

oh. __ Oh, _____ ooh, __ no, __

no. _____

I got-ta get my-self to-geth-er;

I got-ta stop tell-in' my-self that I can do no bet - ter.

I got-ta go out and may-be start meet-ing some new peo-ple;

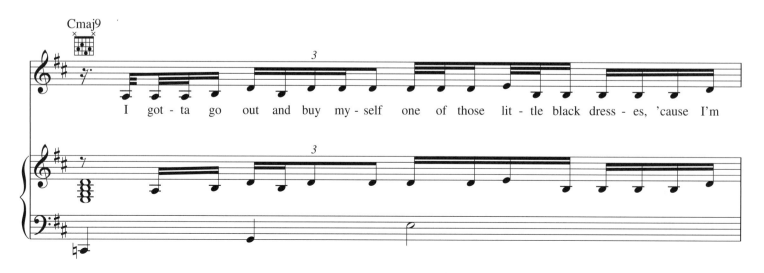

I got-ta go out and buy my-self one of those lit-tle black dress-es, 'cause I'm

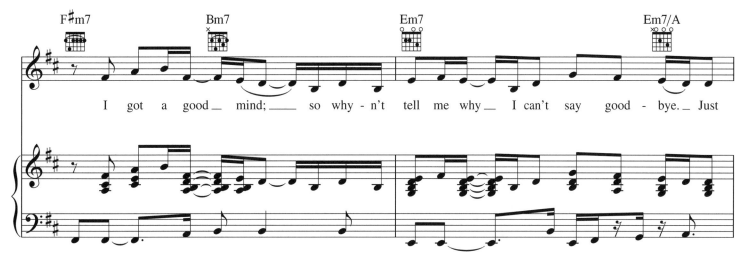

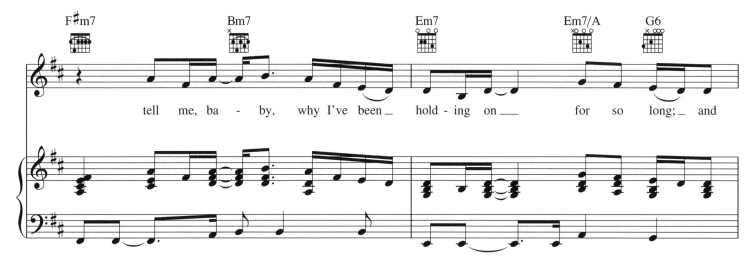

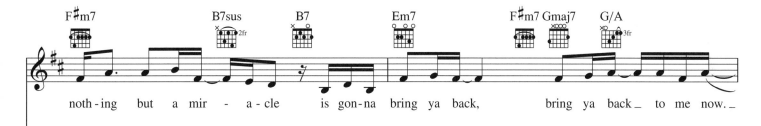

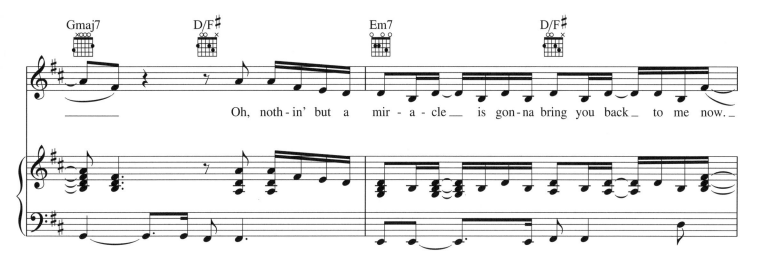

Whoa, noth-in' but a mir-a-cle, _____ oh, no, no, no. _____

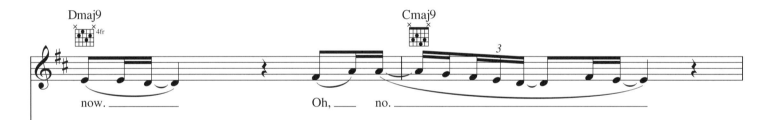

_____ Oh, noth-in' but a mir-a-cle _____ is gon-na bring you back _ to me

now. _____ Oh, ___ no. _____

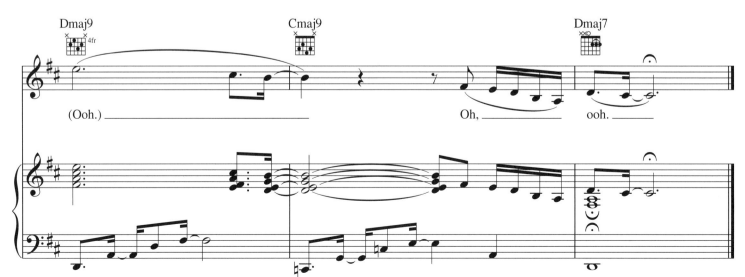

(Ooh.) _____ Oh, _____ ooh. _____

# REWIND

Words and Music by
DIANE BIRCH

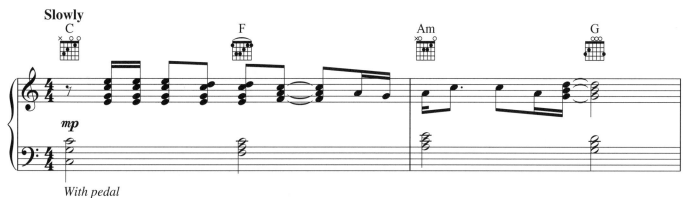

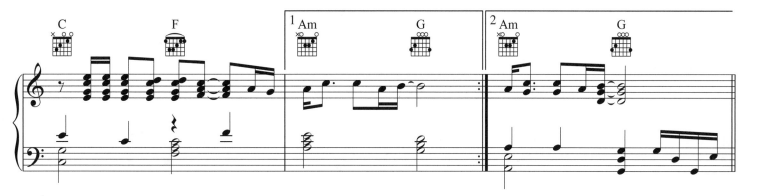

There are man-y things _ that I would like to say _ to you, _ but

I don't have the words in my _ head. _

Days are pass - ing by, ___ and all the leaves are chang - in', too; ___ but

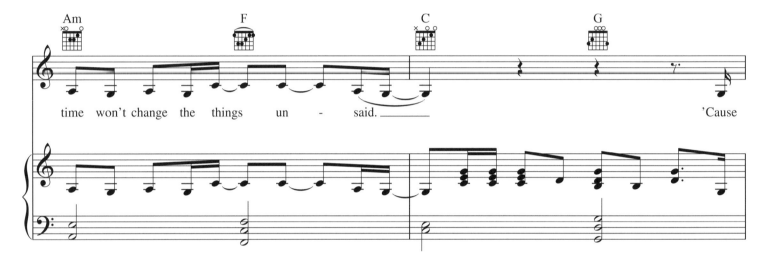

time won't change the things un - said. ___ 'Cause

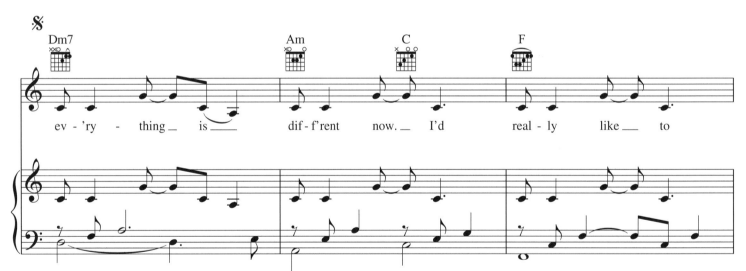

ev - 'ry - thing __ is ___ dif - f'rent now. __ I'd real - ly like __ to

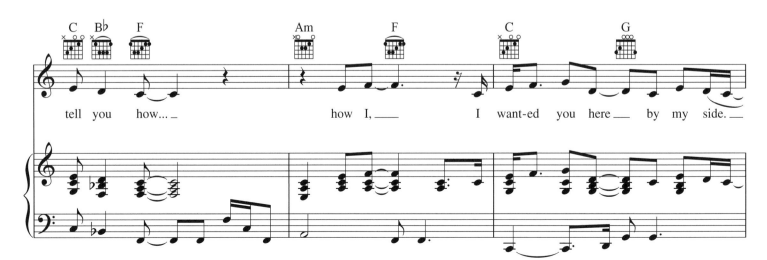

tell you how... ___ how I, ___ I want-ed you here ___ by my side. ___

I know what I said, ___ but I ___ lied. ___

It looked like ___ a laugh, ___ but I cried. ___

Whoa, I ___
'Cause I ___

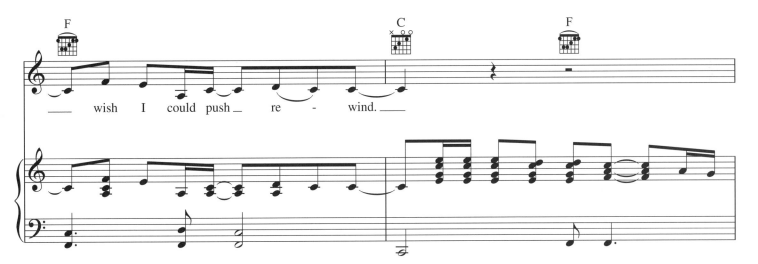

___ wish I could push ___ re - wind. ___

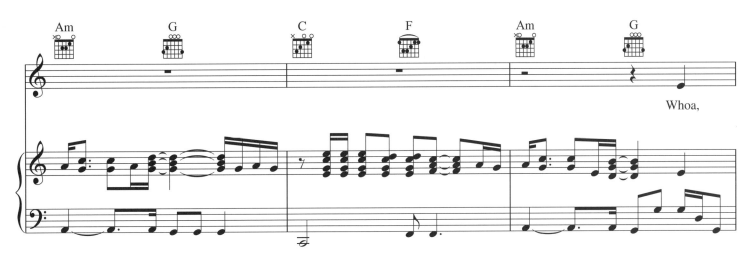

Whoa,

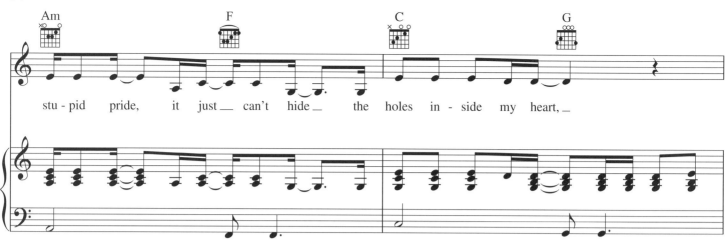

stu - pid pride, it just __ can't hide __ the holes in - side my heart, __

'cause I need you here __ with __ me. _____ Oh, I

wish that I _____ could take __ it back; __ I'd go back to the start __ and

tell you all the things that I ___ feel. _____ 'Cause

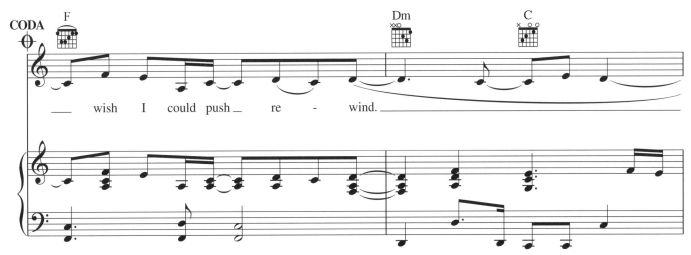

wish I could push __ re - wind. _____

Whoa, __ whoa, ____ yeah. _____

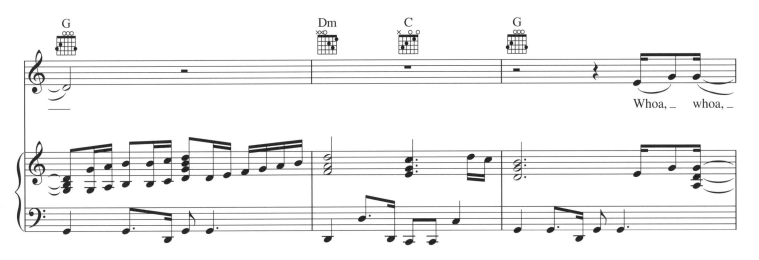

Whoa, __ whoa, __

ooh __ yeah, _____ oh. _____     I

saw you on the cor - ner hold - in' hands with some - one new, __

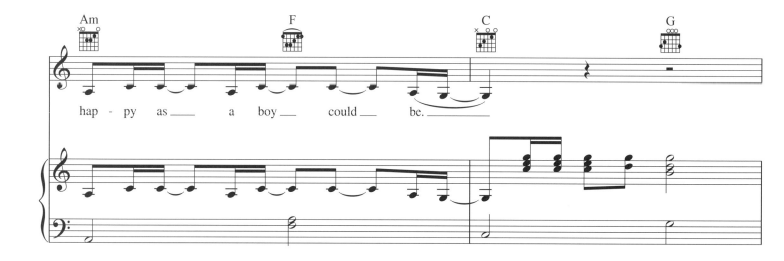

hap - py as __ a boy __ could __ be. __

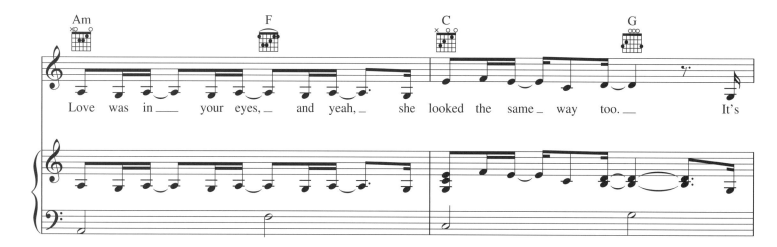

Love was in __ your eyes, __ and yeah, __ she looked the same __ way too. __ It's

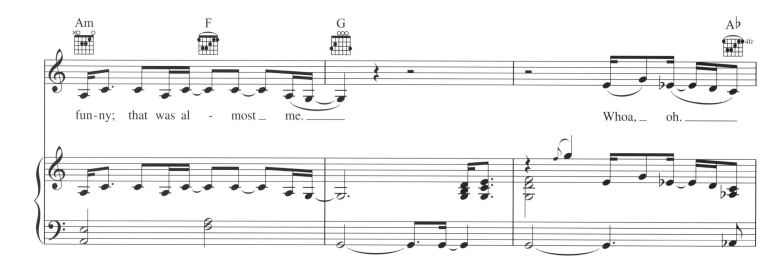

fun - ny; that was al - most __ me. __ Whoa, __ oh. __

Now I, _____ I wan-na be there _____ by your side. _____

I know what I said, _____ but I _____ lied. _____

Oh, I want-ed to laugh, _____ but I cried, _

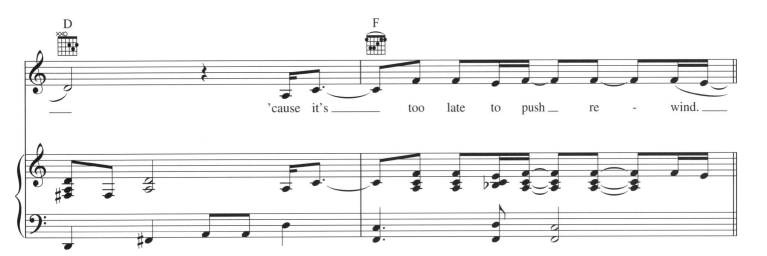

'cause it's _____ too late to push re - wind. _____

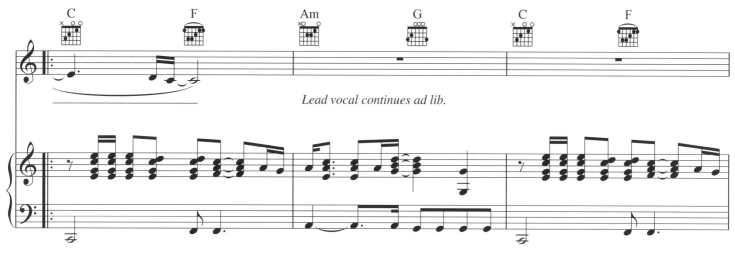

*Lead vocal continues ad lib.*

**Repeat ad lib.** | **Final Ending**

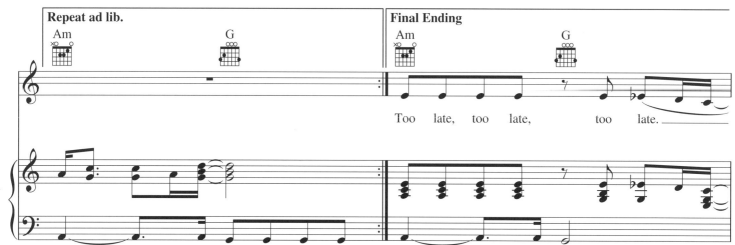

Too late, too late, too late.

I can't push re - wind.

Oh, no, no, it's too late.

# RISE UP

Words and Music by
DIANE BIRCH

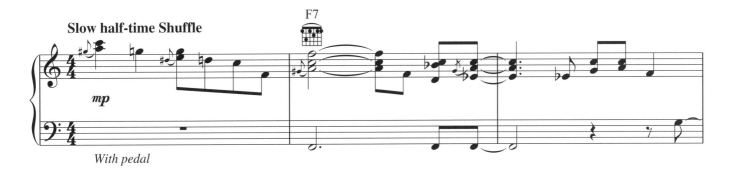

Why not say it like it is,

like you know you should, ___ be - fore they break your ___ lit - tle

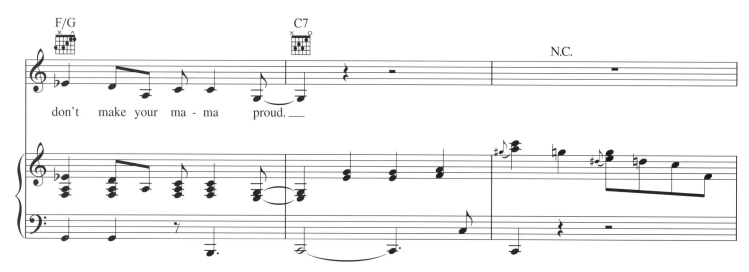

Why change your mind \_\_\_\_ when you make it up? \_\_\_\_

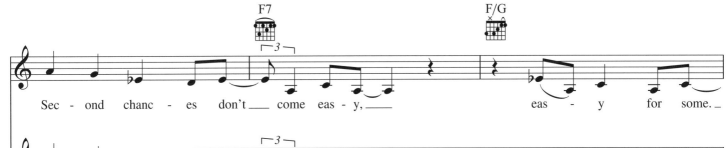

Sec - ond chanc - es don't \_\_\_ come eas - y, \_\_\_ eas - y for some. \_\_

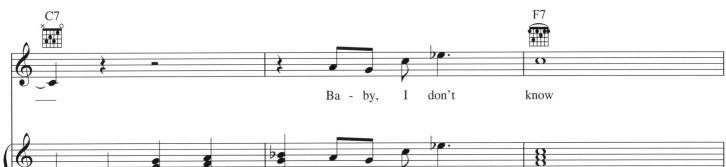

\_\_ Ba - by, I don't know

the lock from the key, \_\_\_ but I know one of them

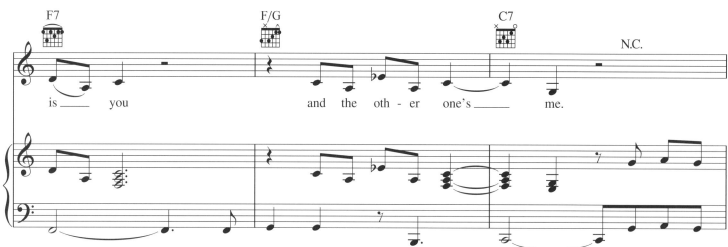

is ____ you and the oth-er one's ____ me.

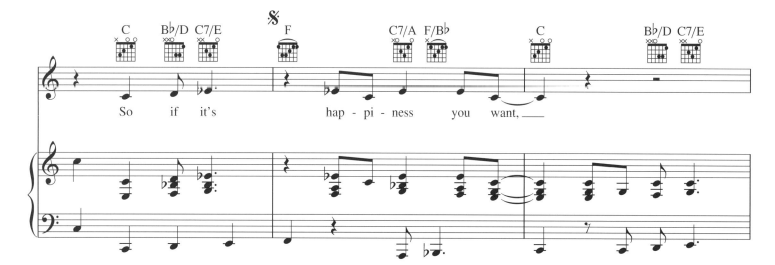

So if it's hap-pi-ness you want, ____

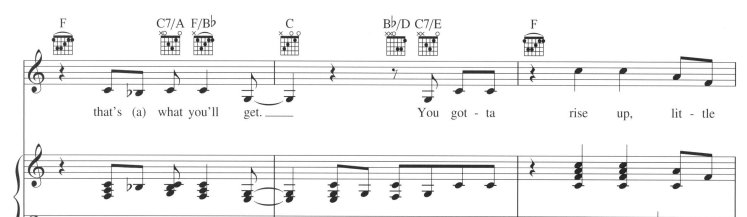

that's (a) what you'll get. ____ You got-ta rise up, lit-tle

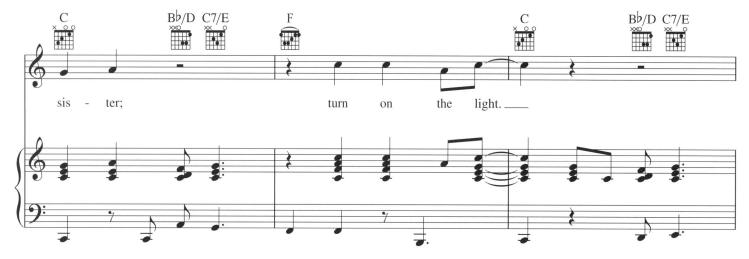

sis - ter; turn on the light. ____

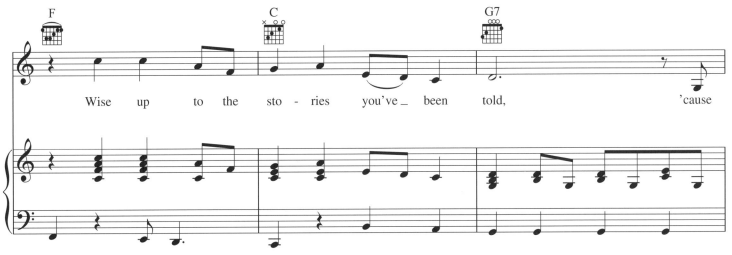

Wise up to the sto - ries you've _ been told, 'cause

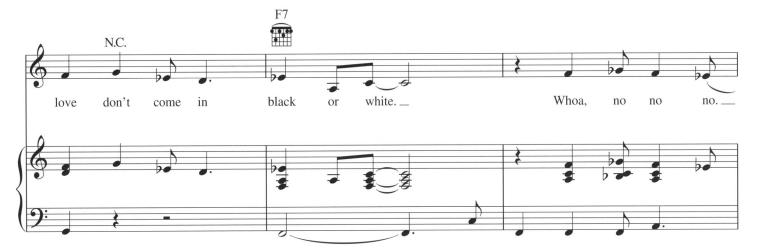

love don't come in black or white. _ Whoa, no no no. _

To Coda ⊕

My ma - ma tells me I won't _ get ___

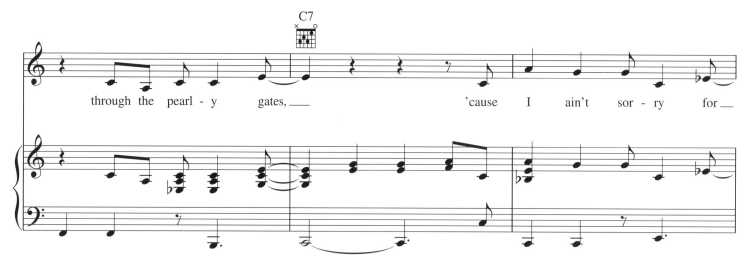

through the pearl - y gates, ___ 'cause I ain't sor - ry for ___

___ my sins and all ___ my mis - takes. ___

Oh, Ma - ma, I don't know if I'm go - ing up or down, ___

but I know Heav - en's gon - na be

D.S. al Coda

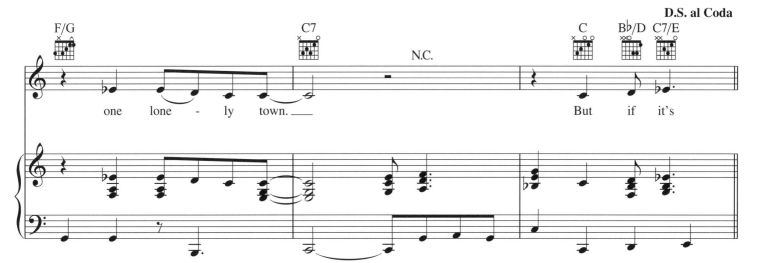

one lone - ly town. ___ But if it's

(Oh, oh, _____

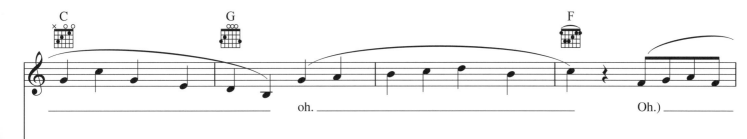

oh. _____ Oh.) _____

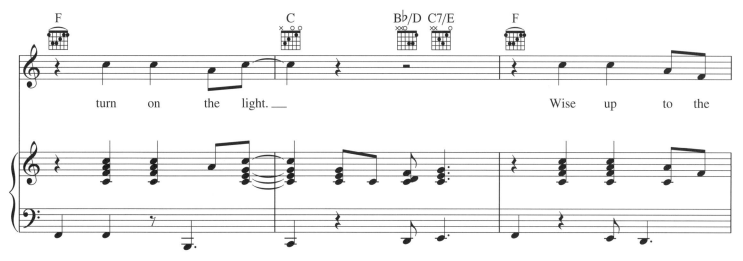

turn on the light. ___ Wise up to the

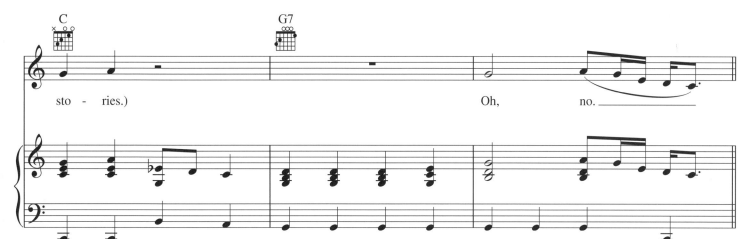

sto - ries.) Oh, no. ___

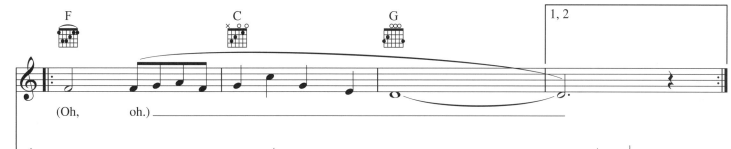

(Oh, oh.) ___

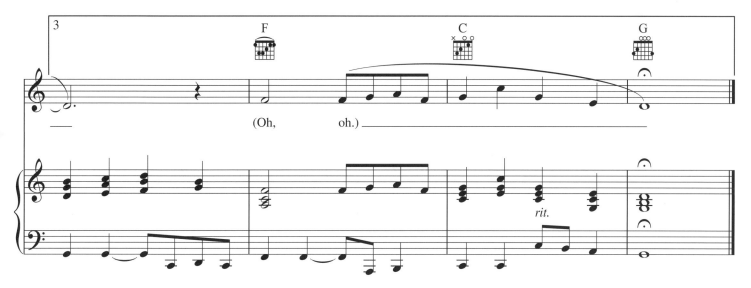

(Oh, oh.) ___

# PHOTOGRAPH

Words and Music by
DIANE BIRCH

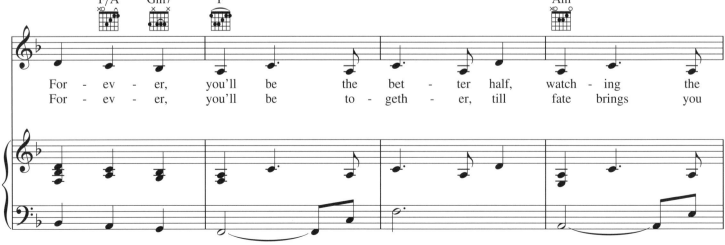

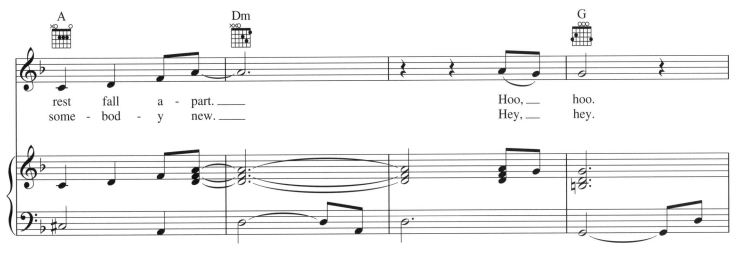

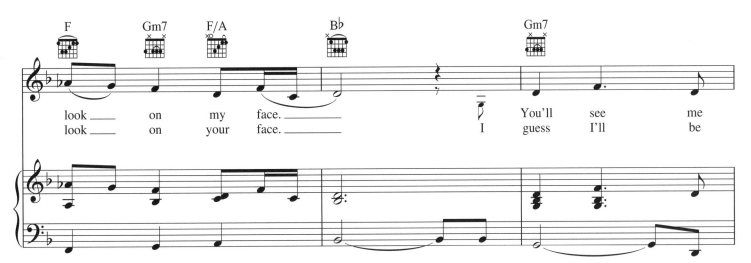

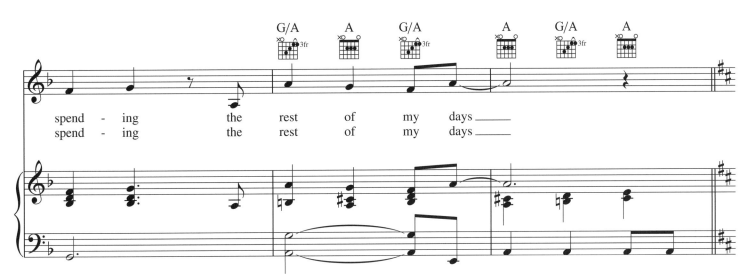

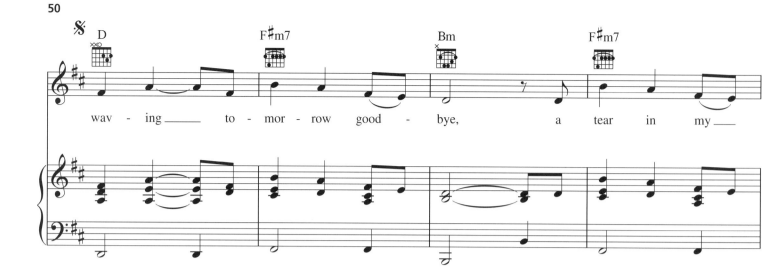

wav - ing \_\_\_\_\_ to - mor - row good - bye, a tear in my \_\_\_\_\_

eye; noth - ing can bring back that feel - ing.

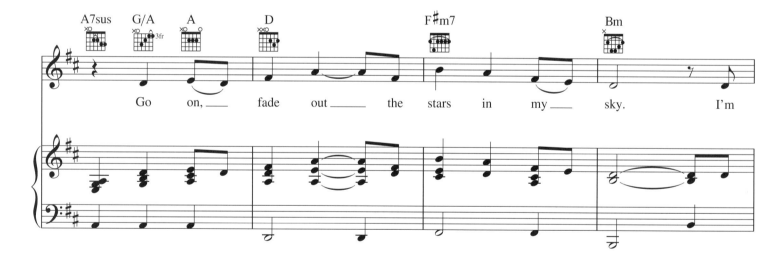

Go on, \_\_\_\_\_ fade out \_\_\_\_\_ the stars in my \_\_\_\_\_ sky. I'm

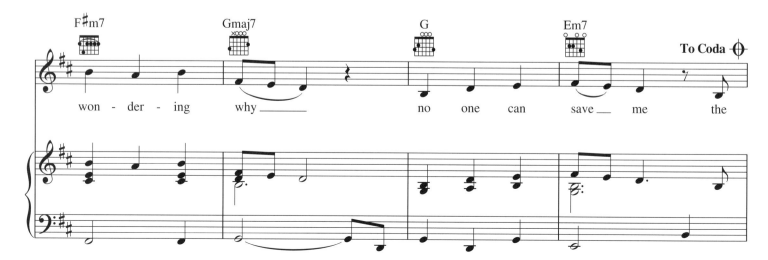

won - der - ing why \_\_\_\_\_ no one can save \_\_\_\_ me the

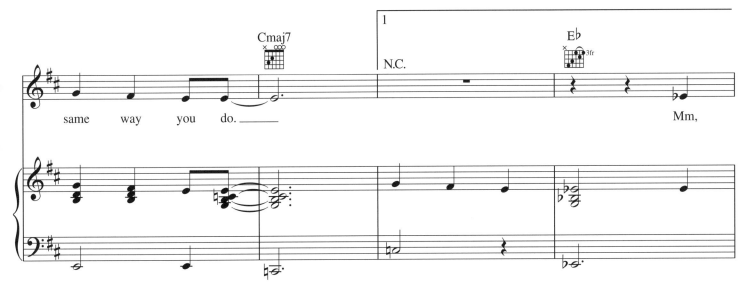

same way you do. _____ Mm,

hmm. _____

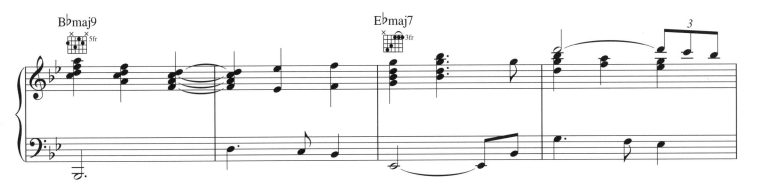

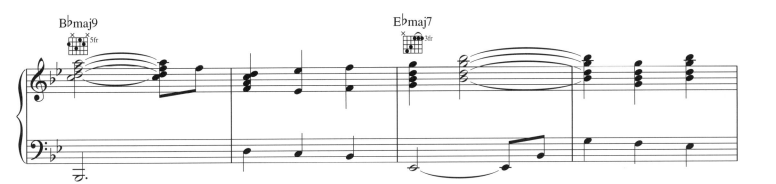

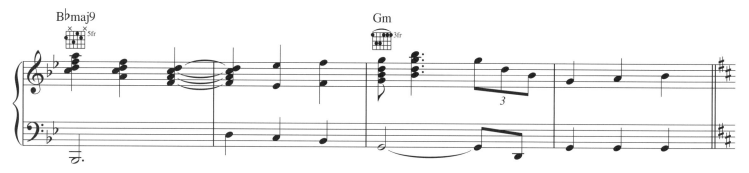

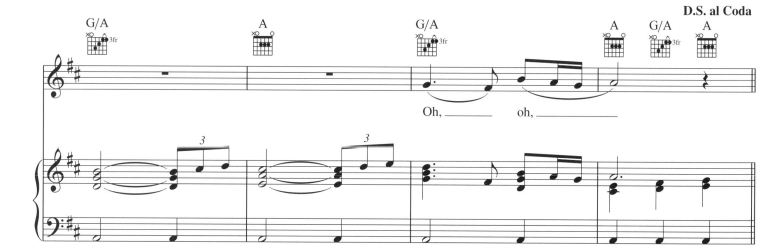

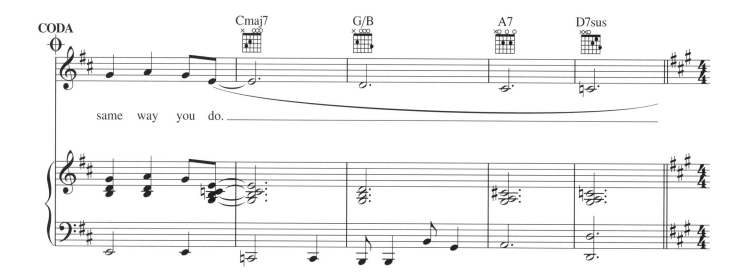

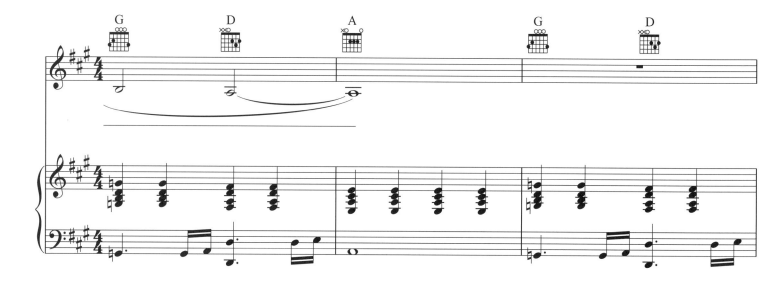

# DON'T WAIT UP

*Instrumental solo*

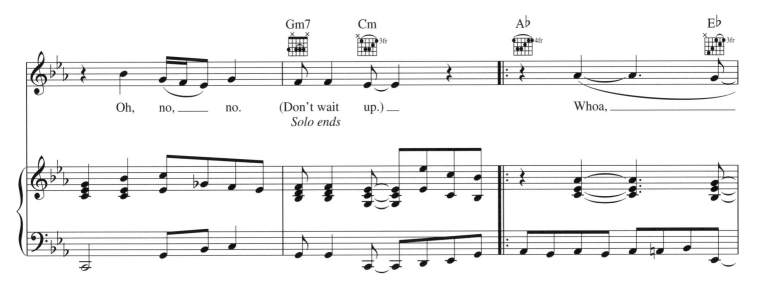

Oh, no, ____ no. (Don't wait up.) ____ Whoa, ____
*Solo ends*

____ oh, don't wait ____ up for me. ____

58

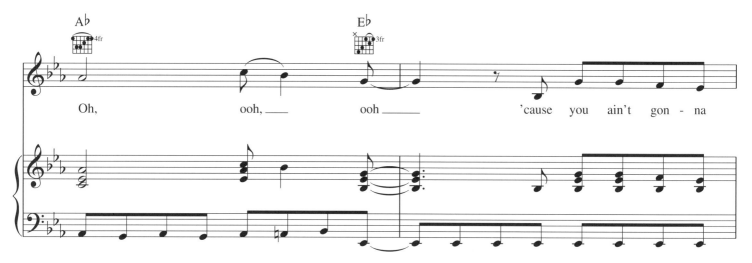

# MIRROR MIRROR

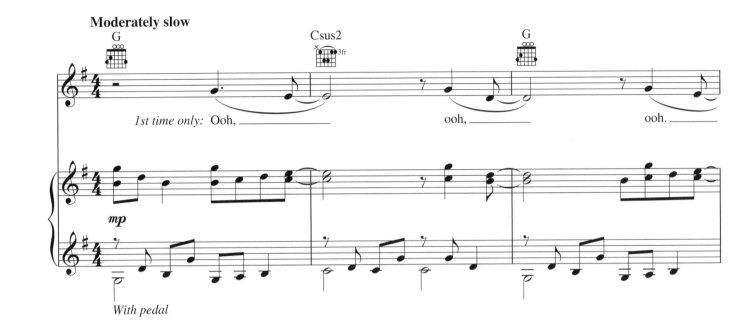

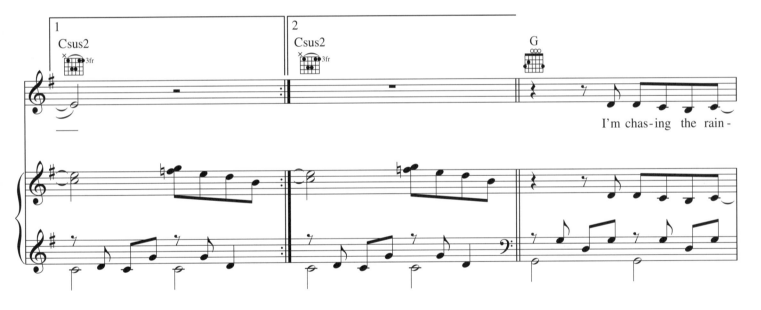

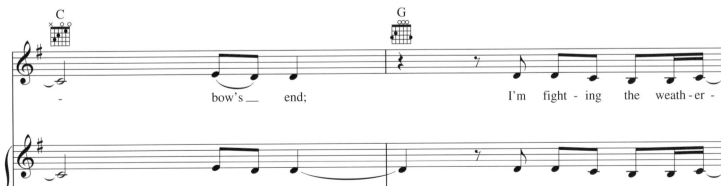

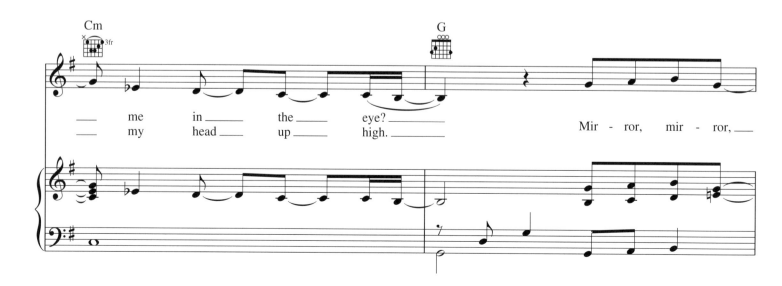

is it me __ or you __ that's ly - ing?

Mir - ror, mir - ror, ___ is it me __ or you __ that's cry -

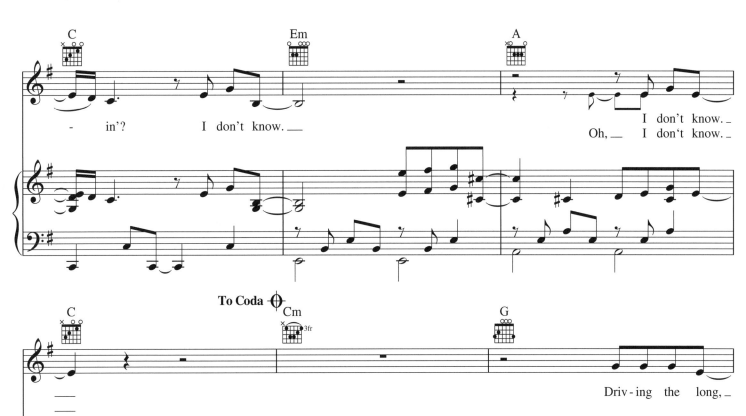

- in'? I don't know. __   I don't know. __
Oh, __ I don't know. __

**To Coda**

Driv - ing the long, __

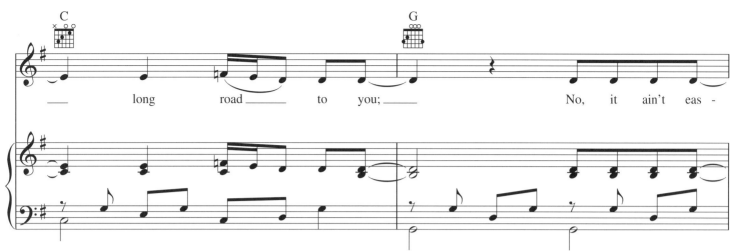

long road _____ to you; _____ No, it ain't eas -

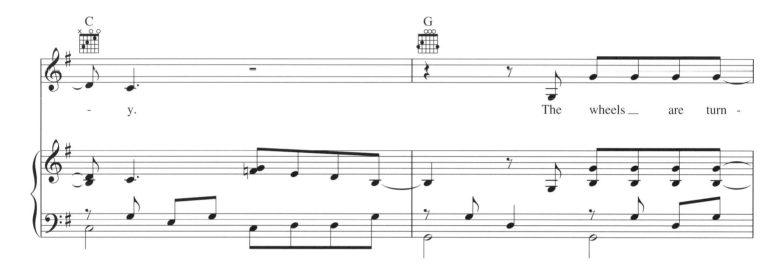

- y. The wheels ___ are turn -

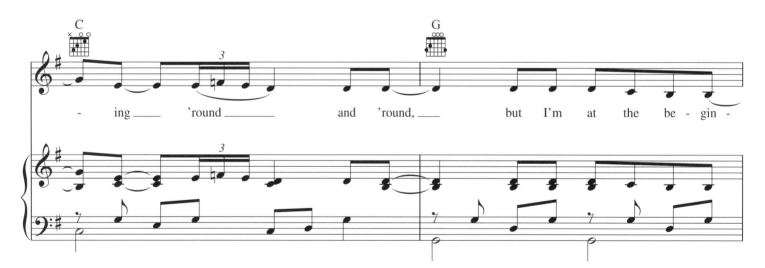

- ing ___ 'round _____ and 'round, ___ but I'm at the be - gin -

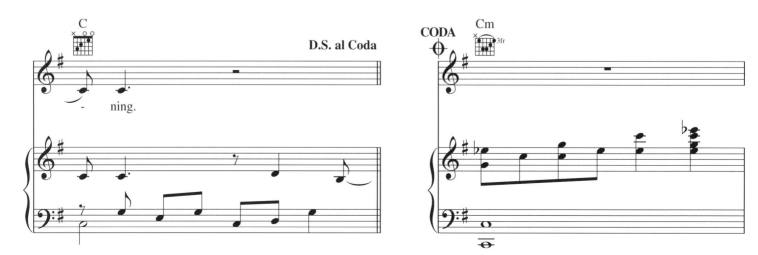

- ning.

**D.S. al Coda**

**CODA**

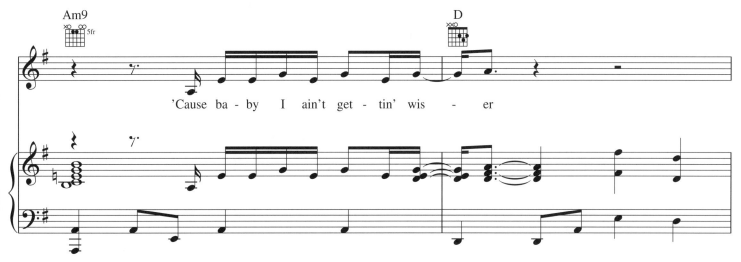

'Cause ba - by I ain't get - tin' wis - - er

tryin' to find that old ___ road to yes - ter - day. ___

Don't you know, ___ I'm on - ly get - tin' old - - er,

watch - in' ev - 'ry mo - ment blow - in' like a feath - er in the

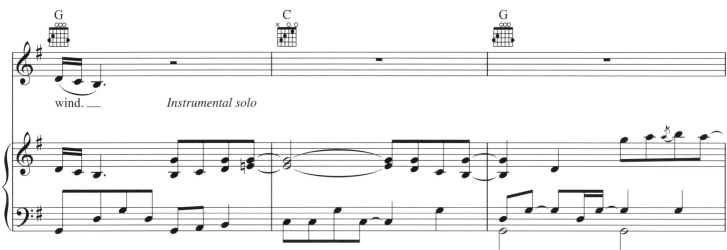

wind. ___ *Instrumental solo*

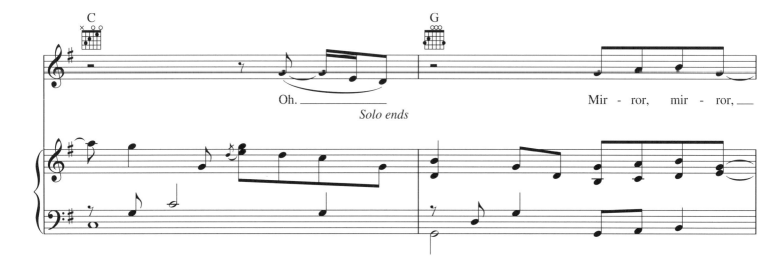

Oh. _____ *Solo ends*

Mir - ror, mir - ror, ___

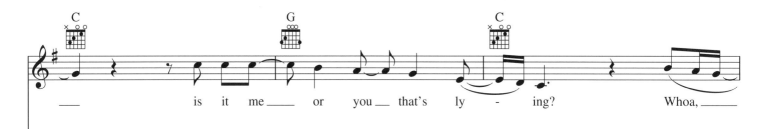

___ is it me ___ or you ___ that's ly - ing? Whoa, ___

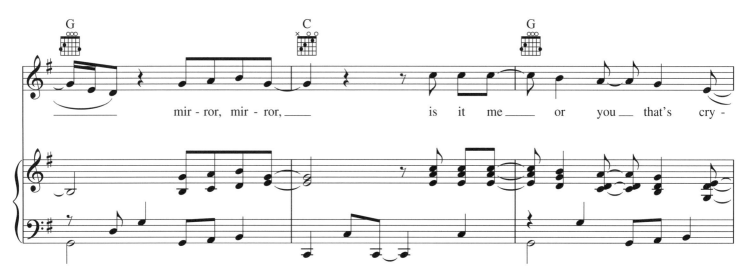

mir - ror, mir - ror, ___ is it me ___ or you ___ that's cry -

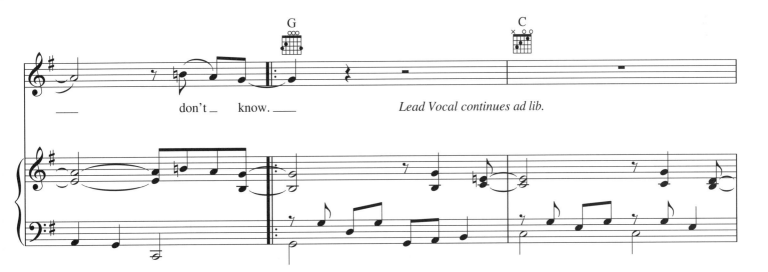

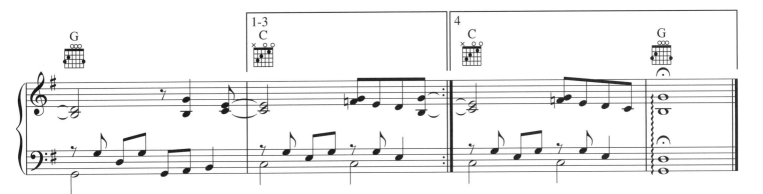

# ARIEL

Words and Music by
DIANE BIRCH

**Moderately slow**

Look-in' 'round for a dif-f'rent high __ in the land of the liv - ing;

tryin' to free the bird __ in - side __ this __ cage. I got

news to-day___ that you're gon-na go___ see the Great Wall of Chi - na. I

guess I'll see all the pic - tures on___ your___ page.___ No

I can't tell the rea - son___ from a rid-dle___ and the rhyme;___

I can't see the feel - in's on___ your___ mind.___ You know, it___

feels like we're on - ly liv - ing un - der the same __ sky when the __

__ clock strikes e - lev - en fif - ty - nine. __

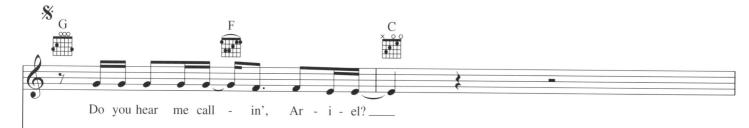

Do you hear me call - in', Ar - i - el? __

Am I a fool to think __ I know __ you __ well? __

To Coda

Do we see the same __ stars, Ar - i - el? __          'Cause

some -times, ba - by, those green eyes just don't tell.

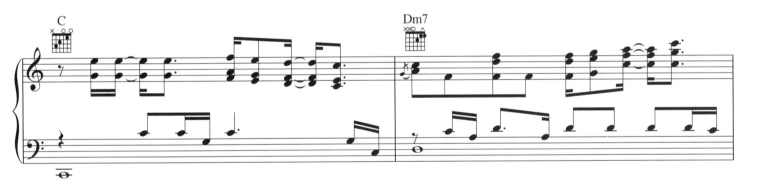

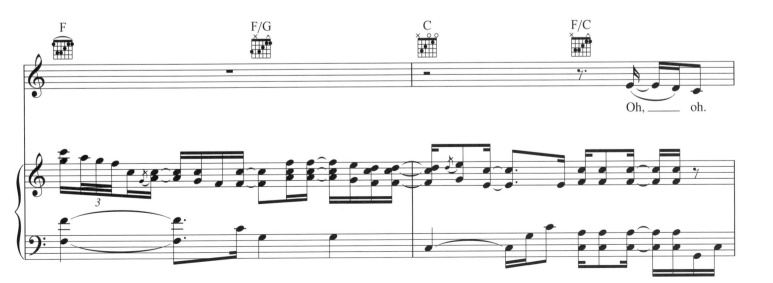

Oh, ____ oh.

I've been cryin' on the pil-low where you lie, \_\_\_\_ for the past, for the fu - ture,

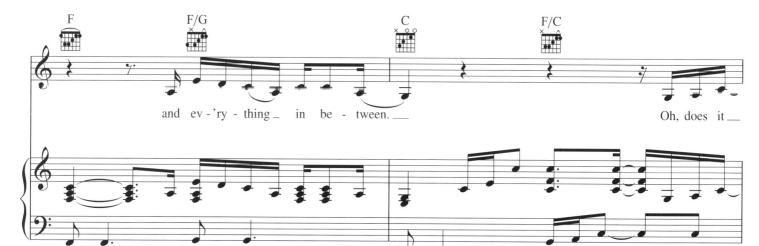

and ev-'ry-thing \_ in be - tween. \_\_\_ Oh, does it \_\_

\_\_ hurt more to lose \_\_ you, or hurt more to love you, ba - by? Or does it \_\_

**D.S. al Coda**

\_\_ hurt more to look at you on \_\_ my \_\_ screen? \_\_

**CODA**

Some-times, ba - by, those green eyes just don't ___ tell.

Are you gon-na leave ___ me lone - ly? Talk - in' to my - self ___ a - gain, ___

look-ing out on ___ New York Cit - y. ___ Do you hear me call - in', Ar - i - el? ___

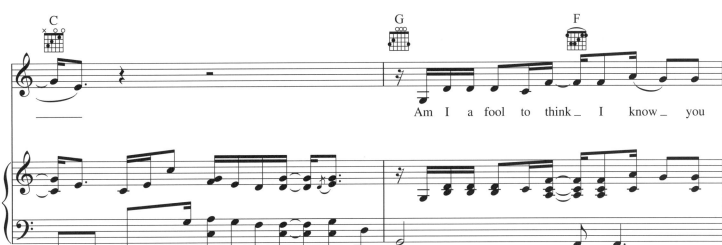

___ Am I a fool to think ___ I know ___ you

well?

Do we see the same stars, Ar - i - el?

'Cause some - times, ba - by, those green eyes just don't tell.

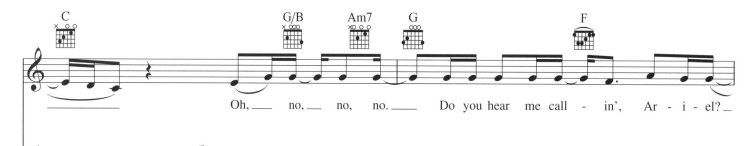

Oh, no, no, no. Do you hear me call - in', Ar - i - el?

Am I a fool to think I know you well?

Do we see the same _ stars, Ar - i - el? _

'Cause some-times, ba - by, those green eyes, _____ they just don't _

tell.

No, they just don't tell. _____

Whoa, _ oh, _ oh. _____

# CHOO CHOO

Words and Music by
DIANE BIRCH

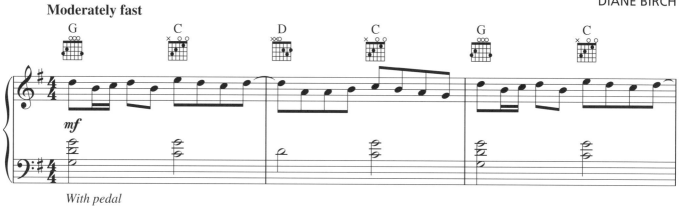

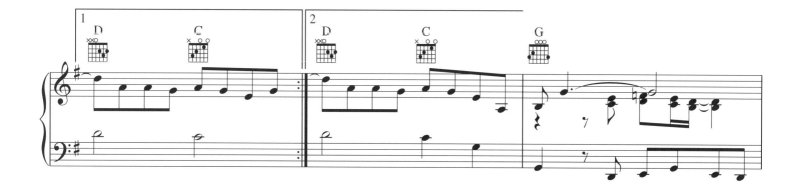

My, my baby's got a cher - ry eye; ___
my, baby's got a heart of gold,
Oh my, my baby's got a talk so sweet;

-en, I see it's just an-oth-er road ___ to hell. ___
-en, but I'm on the choo ___ choo ___ straight ___ to hell. ___

___
___ The dev-il's got my ba - by;

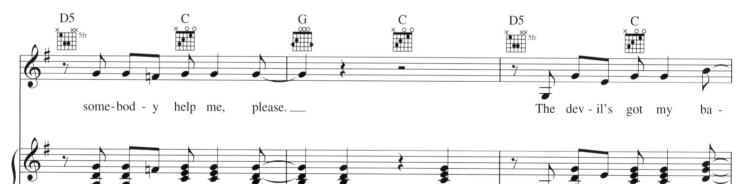

some-bod - y help me, please. ___ The dev-il's got my ba -

- by; I think ___ he's real-ly af-ter ___ me. ___

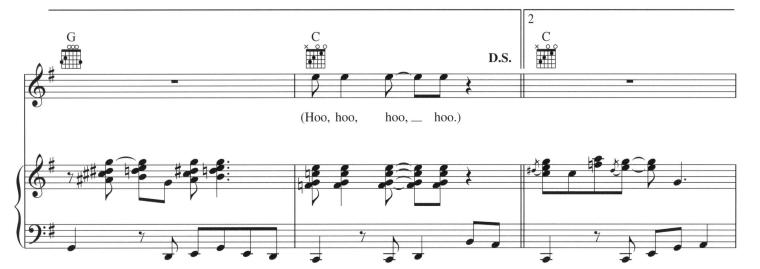

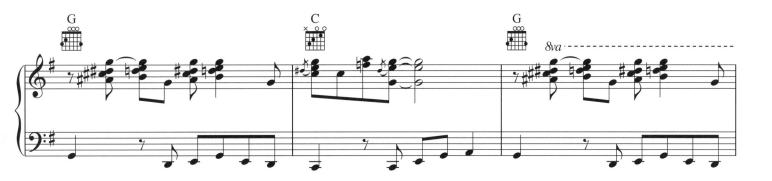

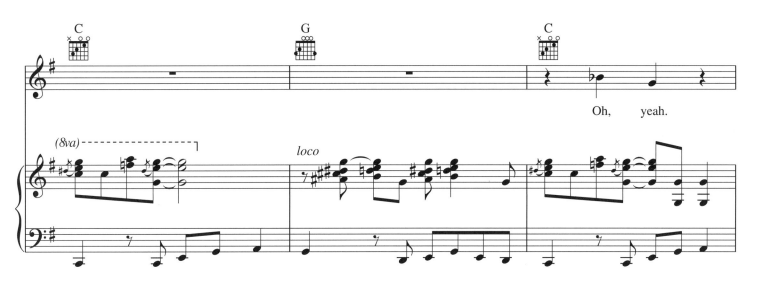

Just when I think I'm on my way ___ to heav-

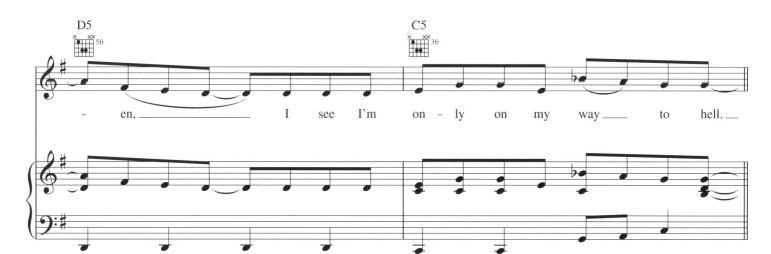

-en, ___ I see I'm on-ly on my way ___ to hell.

___ Oh, ___ yeah. The dev-il's got my ba - by; Oh, ___

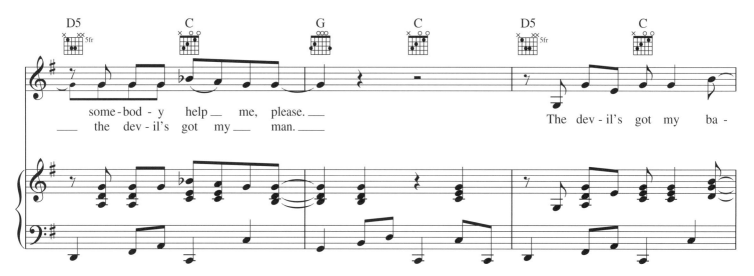

some-bod-y help ___ me, please. ___
___ the dev-il's got my ___ man. ___

The dev-il's got my ba-

# FORGIVENESS

Words and Music by
DIANE BIRCH

Slowly

Hal - le -

With pedal

lu - jah.
lu - jah.
lu - jah.

F7

I got wat - er;
I got flow - ers
You're a sin - ner;

Bb

Bb7

I got
in my
you're a

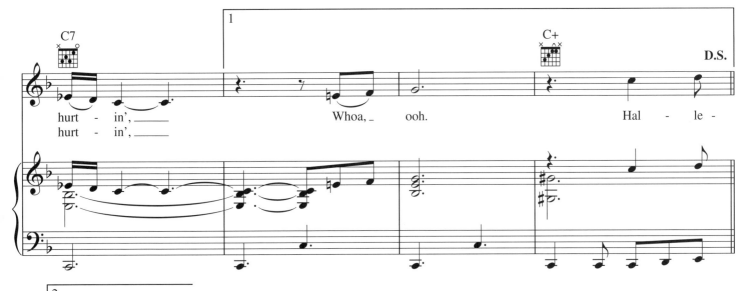

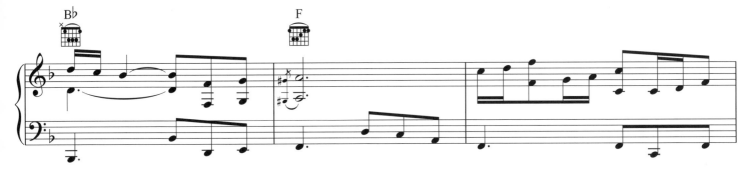

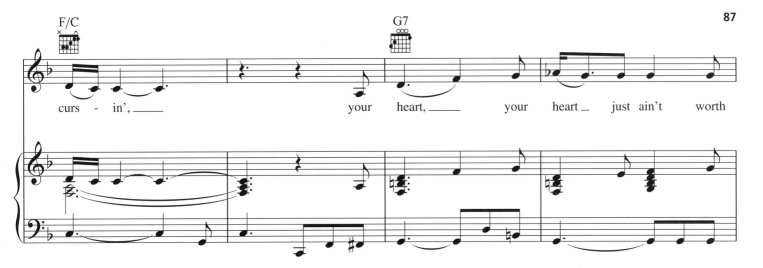

curs - in', \_\_\_\_ your heart, \_\_\_\_ your heart \_\_ just ain't worth

hurt - in'. \_\_\_\_ Ah, _____ ooh. _____

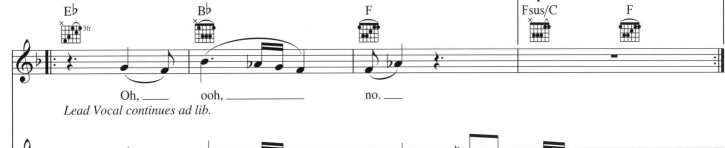

**Repeat and Fade**

Oh, \_\_\_ ooh, _____ no. \_\_
*Lead Vocal continues ad lib.*

**Optional Ending**

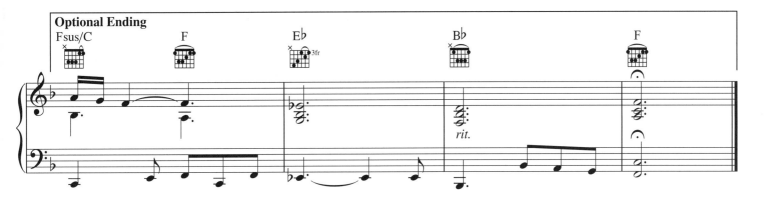

*rit.*

# MAGIC VIEW

Words and Music by
DIANE BIRCH

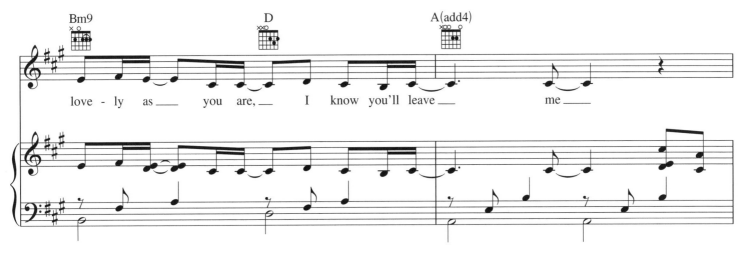

love - ly as ___ you are, ___ I know you'll leave ___ me ___

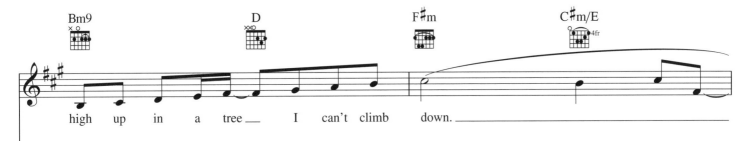

high up in a tree ___ I can't climb down. ___

But I don't mind the trou - ble; it's a

mag - ic view ___ star - in' at ___ the pave - ment un - der

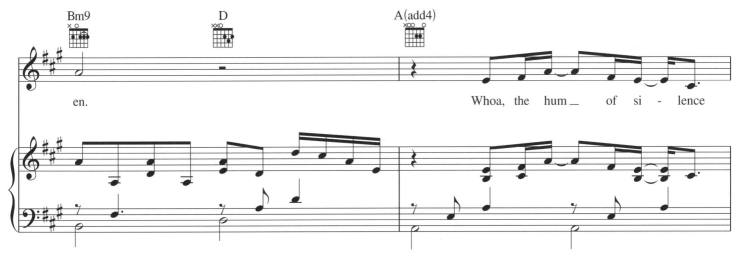

en.                           Whoa, the hum __ of si - lence

nev - er seemed __ so far, but Lord, __ it's        qui - et in ___ my ___

heart.          And I don't e - ven miss      a sin - gle blade of grass; __

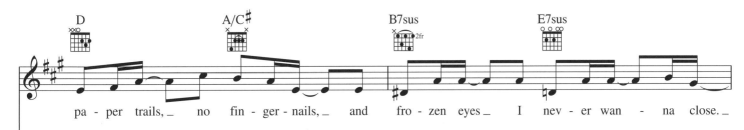

pa - per trails, __ no fin - ger - nails, __ and fro - zen eyes __ I nev - er wan - na close. __

Whoa, _____ ooh. _____

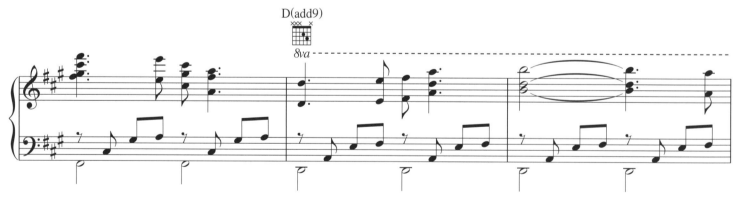

I would be a fool to miss this

mag - ic view, star - in' at the ceil - ing next to you.

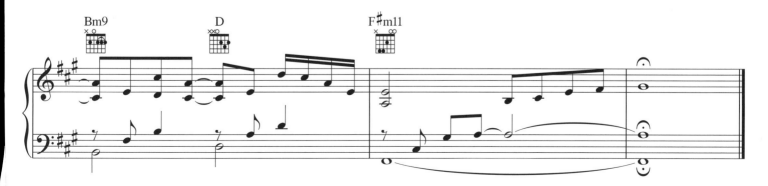